100 Cool Things About Zombies

Shirley Siluk

Copyright © 2013, 2014 freetothink books

All rights reserved.

ISBN: 0692243909

ISBN-13: **978-0692243909** (freetothink books)

FOR NOAH

CONTENTS

	Introduction	i
1	Who First Thought of Zombies?	1
2	Night of the Living Dead Animals	4
3	Rising from the Headlines	7
4	Zombie Tales	11
5	The Science of Zombies	20
6	Zombies at Play	24
7	Zombie Art	26
8	Zombiewood	29
9	What Zombies Can Teach Us	32
10	Survival Tips for the Zombie Apocalypse	36
Bonus Chapter	The Best Websites About Zombies	39
Footnotes		42

INTRODUCTION

What is it about zombies that makes them so compelling?

The idea of humanity being threatened by mindless, animated corpses with a taste for brains sounds simply monstrous, no more. But zombies have inspired thoughtful novels, serious academic studies into the nature of consciousness, soul-searching social commentaries and movies that run the gamut from disgusting to terrifying to hysterically funny to downright bizarre (consider the fact that Nazi zombies actually populate an entire film genre). Zombies have become lurching, ravenous metaphors for helping us to understand these strange, fast-changing and troubled times we live in.

It's that wide-ranging and persistent influence that became my reason for writing this book. Zombies, for all their impossibility (how could any half-rotting human corpse with limited brain function and poor motor control conceivably punch its way through a wood-, metal- or concrete-encased grave and six feet of hard-pounded dirt?), speak to something in us. The concept both repels and fascinates us with its implications for the human race: our ancient origins as prey for other, hungry beings; our universal grappling with the mysteries of death; our essential questions about who we are, why we are and what makes us human.

Whether you're already a fan of zombies, or just curious about why others are, I hope this book will provide a thought-provoking exploration – brain food, if you will – of the subject.

Bon appetit!

1 WHO FIRST THOUGHT OF ZOMBIES?

We can thank Haiti and Africa for giving the name "zombie" to the imaginary living dead creature without any will of its own. But other cultures have also told stories of beings that came back from the grave to torment the living.

For example, the online Zombiepedia[i] (yes, there is such a thing) describes several other zombie-like creatures from ancient folklore. They include the medieval revenant, a corpse that rose from the grave, usually to seek revenge on someone; the Draugr of Norse mythology – dead Vikings that came back to life with super-strength and size (as well as an appetite for living humans); and the ancient Chinese Jiang Shi (which means "stiff corpse"), which could silently hop long distances and could be distracted from attacking human victims by throwing rice or coins to the ground in front of them.

2. The word "zombie" has been traced to two words, the Haitian Creole word "zonbi" and the North Mbundu (a West African language) word, "nzumbe."

3. The concept of zombies originates from the Haitian religion known as "Vodou" or "Voodoo." The religion says that a sorceror known as a "bokor" can bring a dead person back to life. However, dead people who are revived this way have no will of their own: they are completely under the sorceror's control.

4. In the West African Vodun religion, which is related to Haitian Vodou, a sorceror can capture part of a human's soul and keep it in a bottle as a "zombi astral." The sorcerer could then sell the bottle to someone who wanted good luck or health.

5. Fortunately for the zombi astral, its soul wasn't trapped in the bottle forever. The Vodun religion says God will take the soul back after a period of time.

6. According to Haitian Vodou tradition, you can make a zombie go back to the grave by feeding it salt. The salt would "wake up" the zombie from its zombie trance, leading it to abandon the person

controlling it.

7. In old Haiti, zombies were actually believed to be helpful to some humans. Some people believed that rich farmers were successful because they had many zombies working for them in the fields.[ii]

8. Many stories of "real-life" zombies in old Haiti probably stemmed from encounters with people who were odd, sick or mentally ill. For example, a psychiatrist who worked in Haiti in the 1940s recounted the story of a strange woman who showed up in a village wearing rags and talking nonsense. Villagers became convinced she was a local who had died many years before, returned in zombie form. The psychiatrist, who brought the woman to a hospital for treatment of malnutrition and other ailments, concluded she probably had schizophrenia, a brain disorder that wasn't understood by the superstitious community.

9. In South Africa, poor rural people as recently as the 1980s told stories of "witches trains" that traveled along streambeds instead of railroad tracks. All the passengers and workers aboard these trains were believed to be zombies, and people out wandering alone at night were in danger of being captured, killed and forced to join the train crew as zombies.

10. In South African tales, all zombies are believed to be a little over three feet tall, have "an infinite capacity for hard work" and eat only maize (a type of corn) porridge.

2 NIGHT OF THE LIVING DEAD ANIMALS

Brain-eating human zombies make for great spooky stories, but being "zombified" is a real threat for some insects. One kind of fungus, for example, has been "zombifying" ants for at least 48 million years. The fungus forces infected ants to march down from their nests high in jungle trees to leaves just above the ground. The infection then makes the ants bite down on a low-hanging leaf, where they continue to hang until after they die. After a few weeks of growing inside the dead ant's body, a stroma – a clump of fungus seeds – sprouts through its shell, ready to infect the next generation of zombie ants.

12. The parasite that turns ants into zombies has to beware of an enemy of its own: a different kind of fungus that attacks the parasite and prevents it from reproducing and going on to make more ant zombies. Because of this fungus, says researcher David Hughes, "Our research indicates that the danger to the ant colony is much smaller than the high density of zombie-ant cadavers in the graveyard might suggest."

13. One kind of fly can turn ants into even more gruesome zombies. The tiny phorid fly looks for an ant victim and swoops down to lay a single egg in the ant's head. The developing larva takes control of the ant's body, first driving it to walk far away from the rest of the ant colony. As the larva grows and eats the ant's brain from the inside, the ant eventually dies. After that, the ant's head falls off and the next generation of zombie-creating fly emerges to repeat the cycle.

14. A certain kind of virus can turn caterpillars into zombies, scientists have found. Once they're infected, caterpillars are "brainwashed" into climbing up into treetops, where they gradually get sicker and sicker as the virus multiplies inside their bodies. Eventually, the caterpillars' insides melt into virus-packed goo that drips onto the forest floor to infect the next round of caterpillar victims. The good news is that the virus infects only invertebrates ... so we humans don't have to worry about being "zombified".

15. Parasitic jewel wasps turn cockroaches into zombies to provide living food for their babies. The wasp first injects venom into the cockroach's brain, blocking a natural chemical that keeps insects alert and able to move. Then the wasp drags the paralyzed cockroach into its underground home, lays an egg in the victim's abdomen and waits for its baby to hatch. As the larva develops, it eats the cockroach – which is still alive – from the inside out. Nourished on cockroach meat, the baby wasp hatches about a month later, leaving behind the now-dead insect.

16. Ever hear of a zom-bee? These are honeybees that are infected by flies that lay eggs in the bees' abdomens. As the fly eggs develop inside, the bees start acting strangely, abandoning their hives to hang out near lights in a "flight of the living dead." Scientists are studying to see whether the zombie infection is one reason so many honeybee colonies around the world have been collapsing.

17. Scientists studying zombie bees have created a website to encourage people to report new instances of zombie bee behavior. The website is called ZomBeeWatch.org

18. Another kind of parasite preys on poor little roly-polies, those harmless little bugs that roll into a ball when you touch them. (Also known as wood lice, roly-polies are actually isopods, a kind of crustacean.) The parasite, which lives inside the intestines of some birds, gets eaten by roly-polies that like the taste of bird poop. The infected roly-poly loses control of its actions and starts doing stupid things ... like wandering out in the open to present itself as a tasty snack to birds flying overhead. Bird eats roly-poly, swallows the parasite along with it, and the whole cycle gets repeated.[iii]

19. Most of the parasites that turn insects into zombies can't attack humans. But Trypanosoma parasites have long been a problem in parts of Africa. Spread by the tsetse fly, Trypanosoma parasites cause infected people to become confused, develop trouble walking and talking, sleep or wake at strange times and eventually enter what looks like a "zombie-like state." Without treatment, people who develop the disease usually die.

20. A zombifying fungus that's bad for caterpillars could end up being good for people. Scientists have found that an Asian fungus called "Tibetan mushroom" and "golden worm" could be used to develop drugs for treating cancer, diabetes and other human diseases. The fungus is already popular in Chinese and Tibetan folk medicine, and can sell for up to $50,000 a pound.)

3 RISING FROM THE HEADLINES

You know those Emergency Alert System warnings you hear on TV when there's a tornado warning or storm watch? Well, in early 2013, someone found a way to hack into the emergency systems of a few television stations in Michigan and Montana to warn viewers about a zombie attack (not real, of course) in the area. The warnings included text messages along the bottom of the TV screen that reported "dead bodies are rising from their graves" and "attacking the living." Officials weren't sure who did the hacking, but the TV stations changed their equipment to prevent such zombie broadcasts from happening again.[iv]

22. Tracking diseases and warning people about epidemics is serious business. But the government agency in charge of that in the US – the Centers for Disease Control and Prevention (CDC) – sometimes has a little fun with its work. When it decided in 2011 to remind people about how important it is to prepare for emergencies, the agency did so with a downloadable comic novella and a blog post called, "Preparedness 101: Zombie Apocalypse." The post quickly became so popular that the CRC's website temporarily crashed.[v] (The site also offered "Zombie Task Force" t-shirts for sale, but those are no longer available.)

23. So what *do* you do to prepare for a zombie apocalypse? The CDC recommended the usual disaster preparedness tips: 1) Pull together a kit of emergency supplies (water, food, flashlight, battery-powered radio, extra batteries, first-aid kit, medications, cellphone with chargers, emergency blankets, etc.), 2) Have a disaster plan and a place for your family to meet if you're separated and 3) Stay informed and know how to keep a healthy frame of mind.[vi]

24. Like the CDC in the US, government agencies in Canada have also used the idea of an imaginary zombie apocalypse as a way to stay on top of public safety preparedness. In fact, Minister of Foreign Affairs John Baird went so far as to say, "Canada will never become a safe haven for zombies, ever!"[vii]

25. A small horde of young zombies was recently seen wandering the halls of the Rhode Island State House. The "zombies" were actually high-school students dressed like the walking dead to protest a new state graduation requirement related to standardized testing. One student explained, "To take away the diploma is to take away our life, to make us undead."[viii]

24. Zombies might not real, but they've had a big influence on our culture. How big? So big that The Guardian, one of Britain's most influential newspapers, has an entire section of its "Culture" coverage that's devoted to zombies.[ix]

25. How could you possibly improve upon a classic romantic novel like Jane Austen's *Pride and Prejudice*? Add zombies! In 2009, Quirk Books published Seth Grahame-Smith's *Pride and Prejudice and Zombies: The Classic Regency Romance – Now with Ultraviolent Zombie Mayhem!*[x] Booklist's review summed it up like this: "In what's described as an 'expanded edition' of *Pride and Prejudice*, 85 percent of the original text has been preserved but fused with 'ultraviolent zombie mayhem.' For more than 50 years, we learn, England has been overrun by zombies, prompting people like the Bennets to send their daughters away to China for training in the art of deadly combat, and prompting others, like Lady Catherine de Bourgh, to employ armies of ninjas. Added to the familiar plot turns that bring Elizabeth and Mr. Darcy together is the fact that both are highly skilled killers, gleefully slaying zombies on the way to their happy ending." Grahame-Smith, by the way, also wrote *Abraham Lincoln: Vampire Hunter*.

26. Another zombie-loving modern-day author, Frank Swain, recently came out with a book called, *How to Make a Zombie: The Real Life (and Death) Science of Reanimation and Mind Control*.[xi] In the book, Swain – founder of the SciencePunk blog covering "the fringes of science," – explores real-life stories throughout history about "resuscitation, resurrection and immortality." For example, he describes how zombification was taken so seriously in Haiti that "the nefarious practice of creating an undead slave is prohibited in the law books. Article 246 of the Haitian Penal Code expressly states that poisoning with the intent to produce a death-like state – the first step in creating a zombie – will be treated no differently than murder."[xii]

27. Looking for some zombie-related fun? The website Death by Zombie[xiii] lets you find a zombie walk, film festival or other undead event somewhere near you. It also features photos, makeup how-tos, links to games and videos, and a list of suggested ways to kill a zombie. (Tip number 1: flamethrower.)

28. What personality type are you – zombie or vampire? A 2011 New York Times article[xiv] devoted two whole pages to describing the traits that make you one or another: vampires live and work alone, zombies travel in packs; vampires can charm, while charm means nothing to the ruthlessly efficient, impersonal zombie. According to the article, Steve Jobs of Apple was a vampire; Bill Gates of Microsoft is a zombie. Twitter is for vampires. Facebook is for zombies.

29. What are the safest countries to be in when the zombie apocalypse strikes? The Zombie Research Society (yes, there really is such a thing) says it will help to be in a country with a low population density (so you're not as likely to run into zombie hordes). Countries with strong militaries or where people are used to tough living conditions are also good. The society's top 10 list? 1) Australia, 2) Canada, 3) US, 4) Russia, 5) Kazakhstan, 6) Bolivia, 7) Norway, 8) Finland, 9) Argentina and 10) Sweden.[xv]

30. Using an online tool called Map of the Dead – Zombie Apocalypse Survival,[xvi] you can search any area by city, address or postal code to locate supplies and the best places to avoid should the walking dead start rising hungry from their graves. Use it to find the nearest fire station ("Probably has plenty of first aid supplies … and axes!"), harbor ("Find a boat and escape to an island.") or cemetery ("Likely a low-risk location, as the undead are trapped underground. But still super creepy."). Map of the Dead also has an iPhone game app.

4 ZOMBIE TALES

In his book *How to Make a Zombie*, Frank Swain recounts a story reported by Harper's Magazine writer Lafcadio Hearn in 1889 following a visit to Haiti. The daughter of a woman from whom Hearn had rented a room told him the tale of "a harmless simpleton" named Baidaux, who for years talked about a child he had. Baidaux's sister didn't believe him, the story went, until he returned one day leading a small boy by the hand:

" 'Every day I have been telling you I had a child, you would not believe me,' he told the sister, 'Very well, look at him!' She looked, and saw that the child was growing taller and taller, right before her eyes. She threw open the shutters and screamed to her neighbours for help. The towering child turned to Baidaux and told him, 'You are lucky that you are mad!' When the neighbours came running in, they found nothing; the zombie had vanished."

32. Some say the legendary musician Jelly Roll Morton – born in New Orleans sometime around 1889 – was a "jazz zombie."

After being kicked out of his grandmother's house for playing "devil music," Morton went to live with his godmother. She was a voodoo queen, according to Jerry Gandolfo, owner of the New Orleans Voodoo Museum.[xvii]

"Every time Morton's career went south, Gandolfo explained, the godmother fixed things. An example: During the Great Depression, he gets a knock on the door and it's RCA Victor wanting to sign him. Legend has it, Gandolfo said, that Morton, to further his career, relinquished his soul to his godmother, who kept it in a jar. Who knows? But, Gandolfo said, one thing's sure: Four days after the godmother died, Morton died — of no apparent cause. Souls in jars, Gandolfo said, have to be fed."

33. Zombie stories aren't just spooky tales from long ago: The Daily Sun newspaper in South Africa reported in July 2013 that a couple – Caroline and Vusi – had bought their dream home from an old woman (often called a "gogo"), only to discover the house outside of

Johannesburg was haunted by "zombie spirits"[xviii]:

> "There were sounds of footsteps and people running around and fighting and hitting each other with chairs, even 'the rhythmic sounds of dancing feet,' the paper reported.
>
> " 'Neighbours said the gogo had six kids – five boys and one girl – but the boys died one after the other. Only the girl was left behind,' said Caroline. 'She is the one who sold us the house.'
>
> "When Daily Sun contacted the seller of the house, she confirmed that her siblings had all died. 'I told them not to open the door. That was my mother's bedroom,' she said. Traditional healer Daniel Mkhwanazi said the gogo probably killed her children and turned them into zombies and they keep coming back."

34. Myths from many cultures tell the story about someone who goes to the land of the dead to try and bring back a loved one who has died. (And the stories usually didn't end well.)

Greek mythology tells of the musician and prophet Orpheus, who tries unsuccessfully to rescue his dead wife Eurydice from the underworld.

In ancient Japan, a similar story was told about the god Izanagi-no-Mikoto and his wife, Izanami-no-Mikoto, who died giving birth to their sixth child:

> "Izanagi-no-Mikoto lamented the death of Izanami-no-Mikoto and undertook a journey to Yomi ('the shadowy land of the dead'). He searched for Izanami-no-Mikoto and found her. At first, Izanagi-no-Mikoto could not see her for the shadows hid her appearance. He asked her to return with him. Izanami-no-Mikoto spat out at him, informing Izanagi-no-Mikoto that he was too late. She had already eaten the food of the underworld and was now one with the land of the dead. She could no longer return to the living.
>
> "The news shocked Izanagi-no-Mikoto, but he refused to leave her in Yomi. While Izanami-no-Mikoto was sleeping, he took the comb

that bound his long hair and set it alight as a torch. Under the sudden burst of light, he saw the horrid form of the once beautiful and graceful Izanami-no-Mikoto. She was now a rotting form of flesh with maggots and foul creatures running over her ravaged body."

Izanagi-no-Mikoto screams in horror at the sight and flees. His undead wife pursues him, threatening to kill 1,000 people in the world of the living every day if he leaves her. He pushes a boulder in front of the entrance to the underworld, locking her in, and shouts that – if she does that – he would give new life to 1,500 people every day.

35. In the Caribbean, there are folk stories about jumbees (sometimes spelled "jumbies"), which are not exactly zombies, but have some similarities. Jumbees are a kind of ghost or spirit of someone evil who has died. Like zombies, jumbees can be confused by salt … although in the case of jumbees, it's because they have an irresistible need to stop whatever else they're doing and count every grain.

In one story – "Mr. Leneman and the Jumbie Head"[xix] – a greedy farmer discovers the land he has bought in a place called Shalitamale is inhabited by a spirit that can call up an army of hands. This army of hands rises up from underground, first clearing the land of brush, and then planting a rich field of corn. The farmer, Mr. Leneman, warns his wife not to touch anything in the field. When he is away one day, though, she decides to help him harvest the corn and pulls on one stalk. This awakens the army of hands, which pull up and dispose of all the corn.

Furious to discover this when he returns, the farmer strikes his wife. The hands then rise up again and beat the farmer's wife until she is gone.

Here's how story-teller Yvette Brandy[xx] recounts the rest of the tale:

"When Mr. Leneman realize what he had done, he start a bawling and a wailing and he started scratching he head.

"(Voice from the field): 'A who dat a scratch he head? A who dat a scratch he head?'

" 'It's me, Mr. Leneman.'

"(Voice from the field): 'Let we help Mr. Leneman scratch he head! Big and little, get up, get up! Big and little, get up, get up! No head left here today there will be, no head left here today!' (The hands rise up and scratch Mr. Leneman's head until it is gone.)

"Well, around midnight, if you go walking through Shalitamale, you will find Mr. Leneman's Jumbie looking for he wife, and looking for he head!"

36. In medieval Europe, people believed there was a kind of gray area between life and death, according to Nancy Caciola, a specialist in medieval history at the University of California - San Diego[xxi]. Someone who had died, but had not yet wasted away to just bones, they believed, still had the potential to rise up and come back to life. People who led a good life didn't usually cause trouble, even if they came back from the dead. Wicked people, though, could come back as evil and dangerous beings known as "revenants."

One medieval tale recounts the story of Henry, an "extremely wicked" knight who rises from the dead as a revenant:

"After he had died ... he appeared to many people wearing the sheepskin that he used to wear when he was alive, and he especially frequented the home of his daughter ... He was often felled with a sword, but could not be wounded: he emitted a sound as if a soft bed were being hit."

37. The Icelandic saga of Grettir the Strong[xxii] includes a story about a shepherd named Glam, a big man with "large grey eyes and wolfgrey hair" who takes a job tending sheep in a haunted part of the countryside. Glam was loud, frightened animals and never went to church. "Every one," the saga notes, "hated him."

After insisting upon eating a meal on a holy day – the evening before the Yule-tide festival – when he is supposed to fast, Glam goes out into a violent snowstorm and never returns. Later, the townspeople find him dead, his body black and "swollen to the size of an ox."

After trying unsuccessfully to drag Glam's body back to town, the villagers bury his body where it lay, covering it under a pile of stones. Shortly afterward, trouble begins:

"It was not long before men became aware that Glam was not easy in his grave. Many men suffered severe injuries; some who saw him were struck senseless and some lost their wits. Soon after the festival was over, men began to think they saw him about their houses. The panic was great and many left the neighbourhood. Next he began to ride on the house-tops by night, and nearly broke them to pieces. Almost night and day he walked, and people would scarcely venture up the valley, however pressing their business. The district was in a grievous condition."

Glam continues to wreak havoc on the countryside – ripping people apart, causing cattle to attack one another, smashing horses to death – until the hero Grettir arrives to confront him. After a furious battle, Grettir cuts off Glam's head and lays it between the monster's legs.

Just to be on the safe side, the remaining townspeople take a few extra precautions so Glam doesn't come back from the dead again:

"Then they set to work and burned Glam to cold cinders, bound the ashes in a skin and buried them in a place far away from the haunts of man or beast."

38. The Federal Vampire and Zombie Agency (FVZA) (a joke organization with a very real website) claims the 1935 Category Five hurricane[xxiii] that devastated Key West was actually the worst-ever zombie outbreak in US history[xxiv]:

"Amid the destruction, infected rats began roaming the island, and by morning, the first of the zombies appeared. Many islanders mistook the zombies for dazed hurricane survivors and the plague

spread across the island like wildfire. To make matters worse, the roads and bridges connecting the keys to the mainland had been washed out by the storm. The islanders had no way to escape. Scores of people drowned when they chose to leap into the choppy surf rather than face the voracious zombies.

"Within days, FVZA troops from all over the south converged on Key West in a variety of sea craft. They established a beachhead on the south side of the island and went about the process of extermination. It took three weeks to secure the island. A total of 3500 people were infected and destroyed, an enormous number considering that there was a zombie vaccine available at this time.

39. Clairvius Narcisse, a real person born in Haiti around 1922, is best known for, as Wikipedia puts it, "being a zombie."[xxv] He reportedly died in a hospital at the age of 40, was buried and then reappeared – alive – almost two decades later."

Brian Dunning, creator of the science site Skeptoid[xxvi], tells Narcisse's story like this:

"18 years later, Narcisse suddenly identified himself to his sister in the street and told a shocking tale. He'd been conscious but unable to move or breathe during his entire stay in the hospital and subsequent burial. After three days underground, his coffin was suddenly opened. He was beaten, gagged, forced to take a hallucinogenic drug, and dragged away to face two years of slave labor on a sugar plantation, as one of many similarly imprisoned zombies. He reported being in a dream state with no willpower the whole time. Finally another zombie killed a captor with a hoe, and the zombies all escaped. Narcisse wandered for sixteen years, afraid to return home, convinced that his brother had been behind the plot. Then, upon his brother's death, he visited his sister."

Harvard ethnobotanist Wade Davis argued in his 1985 book *The Serpent and the Rainbow* that Narcisse's tale was plausible: a "zombie powder" made with poisonous tetrodotoxin from the pufferfish could have stopped the man's heart and breathing just short of killing him, Davis reasoned. However, Dunning notes there's a more logical explanation: The man who died and was buried in 1962 probably wasn't Narcisse, and the real Narcisse probably skipped town for all those years because he had some bad debts and several women seeking child support payments from him.

"Perhaps in his later years he had a change of heart and wanted to reconnect with his family," Dunning reasons. "Considering the convenient circumstances, his zombification was a perfect cover story."

40. Writing in the academic journal "Man" in 1945, the medical doctor Louis P. Mars described one real-life case of apparent zombification in an article titled "The Story of Zombi in Haiti"[xxvii]:

"Early in the morning of 24 October, 1936, in the village of Ennery located in the foothills of the Puylboreau mountains near Cap-Haitien, the entire population was aroused into a tumultuous and frenzied consternation when a woman appeared in the streets clad in ragged clothes. She was old, feeble, and stupefied. Her skin was pale and wrinkled and looked like the scales of a fish.

"From all appearances, she had been suffering from eye disease for a long time. Her eye-lashes had almost fallen out; she could not bear the glare of sunlight and, to protect her eyes, she had covered her face with a dark dirty rag. This added to the curiosity and superstitious awe of the people.

"A mass hysteria swept through the entire village. Crowds gathered around to see that strange woman, people began to ask questions, to cast suspicions, and to try to identify her with various people who were known to be dead long ago."

Upon having a chance to examine the woman a few weeks later in a local hospital, Mars saw that – with improved food and care – the woman had started to gain weight and improve physically. She was no longer the otherworldly, frightening being that had wandered into town but, Mars noted, most evidently an unfortunate person suffering from a mental condition like schizophrenia.

"The unusual circumstances under which (people like this woman) appeared in the village, their queer behaviour and their unintelligible manner of speech, induced the people, whose minds were already conditioned to superstition, to believe that Zombis were in town," Mars wrote.

5 THE SCIENCE OF ZOMBIES

Some scientists spend a lot of time talking about zombies. It's not that they believe zombies really exist, but they find it interesting to imagine a creature that looks human (though a bit decayed) and moves around, but doesn't talk, think or act human. If there really were a creature like this, they ask, would we consider it alive? How would – or should – we treat such a creature? What would make such creatures different from us, and how could we tell the difference?[xxviii]

42. This kind of thinking around zombies explores the subject of consciousness. Basically, if you are "conscious," it means that you are aware that you exist, and you have thoughts and feelings. While we usually picture zombies as not having thoughts or feelings – they're just brain-eating "machines," in a way – some scientists imagine that a zombie-like creature could be conscious ... just in a different way different than we are. For example, maybe they're sick with a disease that makes them care about little else than eating human brains.[xxix]

43. Even if they're not real, zombies inspire lots of interesting scientific discussions about real-world problems. For example, a 2011 book called *Braaaiiinnnsss! From Academics to Zombies*[xxx] explored everything from "Evolution of the Modern Zombie" to "The Zombie Threat to Democracy" to "Zombies, Disability and the Law."

44. In early 2013, London's Science Museum held a three-day "ZombieLab" designed to teach visitors about the science of consciousness. The event featured a zombie horde survival test, a "Zombieoke" (kind of like karaoke) talk show and a "Zombie Academy" where people could learn how to walk like one of the living dead.[xxxi]

45. Could there ever be real zombies? Scientists might not see any reason (yet) to develop a walking dead version of a human. But they have had success at making zombie cells ... non-living copies of mammal cells that are identical in structure to the live versions. Where's the benefit in that? Because the zombie cell's shape is exactly the same as the living version's, it can perform some of the same chemistry as live cells. Unlike live cells, though, the

zombie cells can survive very high pressures and temperatures. "Our zombie cells bridge chemistry and biology to create forms that not only near-perfectly resemble their past selves but can do future work," says Bryan Kaehr, a materials scientist at Sandia National Laboratories.[xxxii]

46. Scientists have discovered a kind-of zombie star out in space. These special types of stars – called Type 1a supernovae – are aging suns that have exploded and "died," only to come back from the grave by sucking matter from other nearby stars.

47. Why do zombies freak us out? (Besides the brain-eating killer part, anyway?) Some researchers think it might be for the same reason that some of us think clowns and almost-human robots look creepy.[xxxiii] They theorize that, somewhere between cute stuffed animals and industrial robots – which are clearly not human – and real-life people, there's an "uncanny valley"[xxxiv] of moving, kind-of-human-like things that our minds can't quite process. When our brain expects to encounter a regular human but instead sees something that's close, but weirdly different, our reaction is revulsion.

48. Do the walking dead have to pay taxes? That's a question that Arizona State University law professor Adam Chodorow explored in a tongue-in-cheek – though heavily researched and footnoted – paper titled, "Death and Taxes and Zombies."[xxxv] Chodorow concluded, "A zombie apocalypse will create an urgent need for significant government revenues to protect the living, while at the same time rendering a large portion of the taxpaying public dead or undead. ... Congress should act now to address this looming crisis, before it is too late."

49. Zombies evoke a horror similar to that we once felt from a real-life threat: rabies, "the most fatal virus in the world," write Bill Wasik and Monica Murphy in their book, *Rabid: A Cultural History of the World's Most Diabolical Virus.*[xxxvi] It's a fear of a "viral force that cuts out a soul, leaving a ravaging animal behind." Medieval European fears of rabies, Wasik and Murphy theorize, probably contributed to the legends of monsters like vampires and werewolves. Fatal almost 100

percent of the time, rabies goes straight to the brain, they write, "suppressing the rational and stimulating the animal. Aggression rises to fever pitch; inhibitions melt away; salivation increases. The infected creature now has only days to live, and these he will likely spend on the attack, foaming at the mouth, chasing and lunging and biting in the throes of madness – because the demon that possesses him seeks more hosts."

50. Could life on Earth have been seeded by zombie microbes from space? It's not as far-fetched as it might sound. For more than 100 years, scientists have considered the possibility that life on our planet could have begun with microscopic organisms from elsewhere in the cosmos that landed here via a meteorite or comet – it's a concept called "panspermia."[xxxvii] Astronomer Paul S. Wesson took the idea a bit further in 2010, when he wrote a research paper suggesting that, while cosmic rays would probably kill most living things traveling through space, the genetic information in dead microbes could have still set the stage for life on Earth.[xxxviii] That would be a variation of the panspermia theory Wesson called "necropanspermia"[xxxix] ... literally "all (pan) dead (necro) seeds (sperma)."

6 ZOMBIES AT PLAY

There are 38 different kinds of zombies in the original version of the game "Plants vs. Zombies." They range from the standard, relatively easy-to-kill zombie to the extremely tough Dr. Zomboss, the final zombie that players must conquer. Dr. Zomboss – whose full name is Edgar George Zomboss – takes 1,583 shots to kill in the regular game ... and 3,165 shots in the mini-game Dr. Zomboss's Revenge.[xl]

52. According to the Plants vs. Zombies "Suburban Almanac," Dr. Zomboss earned his doctorate in thanatology, which is the scientific study of death.[xli] His knowledge of "thanatological technology" allowed him to build the gigantic and fearsome Zombot zombie robot that he launches his attack from.

53. The rarest zombie in the original Plants vs. Zombies is the Zombie Yeti, a kind-of walking dead version of the Abominable Snowman. It's the last zombie that players encounter and first appears after playing Level 4-10 for the second time. According to the "Suburban Almanac," "Little is known about the Zombie Yeti other than his name, birth date, social security number, educational history, past work experience, and sandwich preference (roast beef and Swiss)."

54. Originally released for Super Nintendo and Sega in 1993, "Zombies Ate My Neighbors"[xlii] (called "ZAMN" for short) requires you to save a cast of neighborhood characters before they are devoured by zombies and a host of other monsters. Named by the Telegraph[xliii] newspaper as one of the top 20 zombie video games, ZAMN is more humorous than gory, with weapons that include exploding soda cans, rotten tomatoes, weed whackers and popsicles.

55. Zombies in the game Minecraft are hostile beings that come out at night, or spawn in dark spaces like caves and dungeons. When killed by players, zombies usually drop a couple of pieces of rotten flesh, which – though disgusting – can be eaten.[xliv]

56. In an early version of Minecraft, zombies dropped feathers instead of rotten flesh when they were killed. Game developer Markus Persson tweeted that, "The zombies drop feathers because I don't know what they should drop, and chickens weren't around back then!" In some versions of Minecraft, zombies can still drop feathers when killed.

57. How many video games with zombies are there? It's impossible to count them all, since there are new ones coming out all the time, but Wikipedia lists well over 100 games "strongly featuring zombies,"[xlv] noting that the list is incomplete. They include everything from "Alive 4-Ever," "Call of Duty 2: Black Ops: Zombies" and "Dead Head Fred" to "I Made a Game with Zombies in It!," the "Left 4 Dead" series and the Wii U's "ZombiU."

58. Zombie Zombie, a ZX Spectrum video game released in Europe in 1984, is believed to be the first-ever zombie video game.[xlvi]

59. If you're into zombies AND want to get in shape, there's an app for that. The game "Zombies, Run!"[xlvii] puts you in a zombie apocalypse and gives you different missions to complete as you run for exercise and listen to music on your smartphone.

60. Nothing goes together better than zombies and ... Little Red Riding Hood? Strange as it might sound, in the 2008 Nintendo DS/DSi video game Little Red Riding Hood's Zombie BBQ[xlviii], Little "Ready to Rock" Riding Hood and her friend Momotarō fight to defend Storyland from an invading horde of the living dead. This game also made the Telegraph's[xlix] top 20 list of zombie video games.

7 ZOMBIE ART

Steven Schlozman, a psychiatrist at Harvard University who likes to talk about zombies and consciousness, wrote a novel about what it might be like to be infected with the "zombie virus" and find yourself gradually becoming zombified. His book is called *The Zombie Autopsies*.[l]

62. So zombies can't think and feel? Writer Ryan Mecum begs to differ. He's the author of a whole series of *Horror Haiku* books, including one called "Zombie Haiku: Good Poetry for Your ... Brains." Written from the perspective of a poet who is attacked by a zombie and eventually turns into one, the book features short poems in the five-syllable/seven-syllable/five-syllable haiku style. Poems like, "Biting into heads/Is much harder than it looks./The skull is feisty."[li]

63. Novelist Margaret Atwood – known for such works as *The Handmaid's Tale* and *The Edible Woman* – teamed up with young writer Naomi Alderman to write *The Happy Zombie Sunrise Home*,[lii] a serial novel about a 15-year-old girl struggling to survive in the zombie apocalypse. In addition to writing books, Alderman also co-created the iPhone app, "Zombies, Run!"[liii]

64. Haitian artist Wilson Bigaud, who died in 2010, has a painting called "Zonbi" in the collection at the Figge Art Museum[liv] in Davenport, Iowa. The painting depicts a man leading three zombie slaves – two adults and a child – in chains.

65. Zombie expert Max Brooks, author of *The Zombie Survival Guide* and *World War Z* (he's also the son of famous comedic filmmaker Mel Brooks), once gave an April Fool's Day interview with Archeology Magazine called "Archeology of the Undead."[lv] In the interview, he suggested that the giant stone heads on Easter Island "memorialize a prehistoric zombie outbreak" and warned that global warming could reanimate zombies who had been sealed in tombs in the Arctic.

66. The Fowler Museum at UCLA recently hosted an exhibit called, "In Extremis: Death and Life in 21st-Century Haitian Art."[lvi] Among the many artworks depicting the living dead were Dubreus Lhérisson's fabric creation "Jan Zonbi" showing a wicked spirit with a zombie slave and Frantz Zéphirin's "The Resurrection of the Dead," a painting of rising floodwaters threatening even the spirits in the House of the Dead.

67. If you're a zombie fan who likes creating your own arts and crafts, Fiona Goble has a book for you: *Knit Your Own Zombie*.[lvii] Featuring patterns for everything from the "classic zombie" to a zombie cop from "Resident Evil," the book includes tips for creating ragged zombie clothing, hanging guts, maggots and dismembered limbs. On the other hand, if you're into dance moves, you could practice your zombie grooves by watching Michael Jackson's classic music video[lviii] from the "Thriller"[lix] album. (It's been voted the "most influential pop music video of all time.")

68. The makeup experts from the zombie TV show "The Walking Dead"[lx] have perfected the art of transforming the living into the undead using everything from uncooked oatmeal and gelatin (good for creating flesh wounds) to corn syrup, liquid latex and facial tissue.

69. Her Universe, a clothing company for female science fiction fans, recently became the official merchandiser for zombie fashion inspired by the AMC show "The Walking Dead." The Walking Dead clothing line[lxi] includes a "Don't Open Dead Inside" hoodie.

70. Even pumpkins can become zombie art under the skilled hands of master carver Ray Villafane and his team at Villafane Studios ("Home of the Most Gourdgeous Pumpkins on the Planet"[lxii]). For the 2012 Haunted Pumpkin Garden at the New York Botanical Garden[lxiii], Villafane and his carving partners transformed giant pumpkins (including one nearly weighing a ton) into a horrific sculpture of a six-foot-tall zombie pulling a harvest of zombie pumpkin heads from the earth.

8 ZOMBIEWOOD

Danny Boyle, who directed the zombie film "28 Days Later," said he used the disease rabies as his inspiration for the zombifying virus called "rage."[lxiv]

72. The 1932 film "White Zombie"[lxv] is considered to be the first-ever full-length movie with a zombie theme. Starring Bela Lugosi – an actor best known for playing Dracula in the 1931 movie of the same name – "White Zombie" tells the story of a Haitian master of zombie slaves who "zombifies" a beautiful young woman for a man who wants to steal her from her new husband.

73. In the years after "White Zombie" came out, zombies became increasingly popular in Hollywood films. Other zombie movies of the 1930s, 1940s and 1950s included "Revolt of the Zombies" (1936), "King of the Zombies" (1941), "Revenge of the Zombies" (1943), "Zombies on Broadway" (1945) (titled "Loonies on Broadway" in the UK), "Valley of the Zombies" (1946), "Zombies of the Stratosphere" (1952) and the infamous (for being such a bad movie that it's considered a classic) "Plan 9 from Outer Space"[lxvi] (1959).

74. Today's popular image of what a zombie is[lxvii] was probably most influenced by George A. Romero's ground-breaking 1968 film, "Night of the Living Dead."[lxviii] Oddly enough, the low-budget movie never referred to the flesh-eating walking corpses as "zombies"; instead, Romero called them "ghouls."

75. By now, zombie movies and TV shows come in more than just one "flavor": There are fast-moving zombies, zombies that can talk and remember their past lives ("Return of the Living Dead"[lxix]), guilt-ridden teenaged zombies re-entering society ("In the Flesh"[lxx]), Nazi zombies[lxxi] ("Revenge of the Zombies," "King of the Zombies," "Zombie Lake," "Oasis of Zombies"), teenaged zombies in love ("Warm Bodies"[lxxii]), and much, much more.

76. "Attack of the Vegan Zombies!"[lxxiii], a 2010 film available as a DVD on demand, puts a weird and campy twist on zombie lore. The

movie tells the story of a couple who owns a failing vineyard and has a spell cast on the grape vines to make them grow. They not only grow like crazy, but start attacking people, turning them into zombies. The DVD cover features the tagline, "Zero Trans Fats Has Never Been so Deadly!"

77. While there have been plenty of adult-type zombie movies featuring zombie kids, there are also kid-oriented zombie films. Recent ones include 2011's "Daddy, I'm a Zombie"[lxxiv] – an animated film made in Spain (where its original title is "Papá, soy una zombie") – and 2012's "ParaNorman,"[lxxv] about a boy who can speak to the dead and "takes on ghosts, zombies and grown-ups to save his town from a centuries-old curse."

78. The US TV show "The Walking Dead" is not only a big hit, but has now also become a source of study. AMC, the channel that produces the show, has teamed with the University of California-Irvine to create online courses as an educational companion to the TV series[lxxvi]. Among the topics to be studied: the "science of decay."

79. Even if zombies aren't real, there have been many real documentaries and non-fiction programs made about them. There's "Dead Meat Walking,"[lxxvii] a 2012 documentary about all the zombie fans who put on ghoulish makeup and clothes to participate in various "zombie walks" around the globe; "In Search of Zombies,"[lxxviii] an episode in a TV series about the supernatural and paranormal; and even The National Geographic Channel's "The Truth Behind Zombies."[lxxix]

80. With so many zombie films out there, you might guess that there are probably a lot of zombie film festivals too ... and there are. There's the Leeds Zombie Film Festival[lxxx] in the UK, the Zombie Feast Horror Film Festival[lxxxi] in Canada, Zompire: The Undead Film Festival[lxxxii] in Oregon, The Drunken Zombie Film Festival[lxxxiii] in Illinois, as well as lots of zombie films on tap at various zombie walks[lxxxiv] around the world.

9 WHAT ZOMBIES CAN TEACH US

Zombies are being used a lot these days to teach lessons about other things we really should worry about: climate change[lxxxv], banking laws, the economy, technology that makes our world more impersonal, etc. Imagining how we would fight off a zombie horde, for example, makes us realize how important it is for people to get along, work together and defend our basic humanity[lxxxvi], says Harvard psychiatrist Steven Schlozman.

82. Becoming a zombie might not be good for your health, but running away from them can keep you mighty fit. One fitness trainer in Maryland even developed a "zombie survival boot camp" to help people get fit by imagining they had to fight off zombies. (It started as a joke, but people wanted to sign up for the course for real.) Workout rule number one in the face of a zombie apocalypse? Cardio, the trainer said. (In other words, "RUN!")[lxxxvii]

83. Studying how zombie hordes grow can help us understand things like exponential growth and the spread of infectious diseases. For example, the STEM (for "science, technology, engineering and math") Behind Hollywood[lxxxviii] project has teamed with Steven Schlozman (the zombie-loving Harvard psychiatrist[lxxxix]) to develop a "Zombie Apocalypse" science-based activity. "The activity gives students an inside-look at STEM careers such as epidemiology by using modeling and graphs that the World Health Organization and Centers for Disease Control use to track the spread of infectious diseases."

84. Bradley Voytek, a neuroscientist, self-described "world zombie neuroscience expert" and advisor to the tongue-in-cheek Zombie Research Society, examines what we know about zombie behavior from the movies to understand what the zombie brain would look like compared to a healthy, living human's brain.[xc] For example, he writes, "Given the impulsive and aggressive behavior exhibited by zombies, it's safe to say that they lack a properly functioning orbitofrontal cortex."

85. In a post at his blog, The Cognitive Axon[xci], Tim Verstynen – Voytek's neuroscientific "partner in crime" at the Zombie Research Society – uses imaging analysis software to picture the brain differences between a "fast zombie" and a "slow zombie."

86. "Beyond serving as mere characters in horror films, monsters reveal the social fabric of how societies construct what is 'normal' at any given time," says John Edgar Browning, an English professor at the University of Buffalo who created a seminar on "A Cultural History of the Walking Dead."[xcii] Browning has also authored or contributed to such books as *Draculas, Vampires and Other Undead Forms: Essays on Gender, Race and Culture*; *Undead in the West II: They Just Keep Coming*; and *Fear and Learning: Essays on the Pedagogy of Horror*.[xciii]

87. Results from a zombie invasion game have helped to give insights into how people behave in crowds and make decisions under stress[xciv]. The game's designers – Nikolai Bode and Edward Codling at the University of Essex in the UK – found that people under stress not only make bad decisions about how to escape danger but are also less likely to reconsider their decisions. "It was striking to find that putting more pressure on players resulted in them sticking to routes they knew already and made them less likely to adapt their decisions to changing situations, even if this resulted in longer times to evacuate," Bode explains. "These results could have implications for the design of safe and efficient evacuation routes in buildings and other public places."

88. Researchers at Carleton University and the University of Ottawa recently tested a computer model for how a zombie infection might spread[xcv]. They concluded that, while quarantines and cures could help, only quick and aggressive action – "hit hard and hit often" – could prevent a zombie outbreak from leading to the collapse of civilization. Another scary finding: this was the result for the traditional "slow zombie," as opposed to the more clever, faster-moving ones.

89. Zombies are good models for many things, concludes John Arquilla, a professor of defense analysis at the US Naval Postgraduate School. Real-life events that have acted like zombie swarms include popular uprisings in Poland, the old Soviet Union and – most recently – several Arab countries; the hacking of millions of peoples' computers by robot networks ("botnets"); and the fall of societies from ancient Rome to Native American cultures. "As models of mass social movements, of ways of cyberwarfare, and even as the basis for allegorical historical analysis, nothing says it more clearly than a zombie,"[xcvi] Arquilla writes.

90. For all the research that's been devoted to zombies, there's one question that no one's really found a good answer to: How does an undead, slow-moving, half-decayed and mostly mindless creature claw its way out of a closed wooden, steel or concrete coffin buried under six feet of tightly packed dirt? In a discussion about just this at the All Things Zombie[xcvii] forums, diehard zombie fans all pretty much concluded the same thing: They can't. On the other hand, the best response to this question at Yahoo! Answers[xcviii] was simple but smart-alecky: "They opened them."

10 SURVIVAL TIPS FOR THE ZOMBIE APOCALYPSE

So the zombie apocalypse has started and you haven't been bitten or infected ... yet. What are the best strategies to improve your odds of staying that way? When this question was posted at the site Quora[xcix], some of the top answers included: Keep a military field medic manual and basic surgical first aid on hand; remember that household water heaters are a good source of clean, fresh water; and hide in a big warehouse (metal walls, no easy-to-climb-into windows and ladders for reaching the ceiling or roof).

92. Wear lots of leather, which is hard to bite through, adds Bradley Voytek, neuroscientist-advisor at the Zombie Research Society. Tall leather boots, a leather jacket and some sort of protective neckwear made of leather "would be very effective against the surprise behind-the-shoulder or ankle-biter zombie bites,"[c] he writes.

93. Hit the water, a lot of others advise. Zombies aren't generally known for their swimming abilities, so a boat or island shelter – with adequate fresh water, food and other supplies, of course – would offer a pretty secure way to ride out the apocalypse.

94. In a post titled "How to Weather the Zombie Apocalypse,"[ci] The Weather Channel offered advice from the fictional Dr. Dale Dixon of the "Centers for Disease Development." Cold weather, the article noted, makes a good defense because – having no circulating blood – zombies "freeze more easily than humans." It also offered a disturbing exception to the "zombies can't swim" defense: "(T)hey can walk through and even underwater, as their bodies have no need for oxygen. In deep waters, they sink straight to the bottom. In fact, the oceans and lakes are now filled with zombies at their depths."

95. Neuroscientist and Zombie Research Society advisor Tim Verstynen offers these "scientifically validated" survival tips, which are based on the facts that zombies aren't very smart, have terrible memories and are easily distracted: 1) Outrun them (and practice parkour); 2) Avoid close combat, where zombies have an edge; 3) Lay low and stay quiet until the zombies have forgotten you're there; 4) Throw something to make noise somewhere else and distract the zombies away from you; and 5) If all else fails, pretend you're one of them and hope they fall for it.

96. Know ahead of time where your best resources are. Map of the Dead[cii] recommends knowing the locations of the closest pharmacy or dentist's office (both good sources of medical supplies without the dangers of a hospital), fire station (which will have both first aid supplies and axes) and harbor (grab a boat and set sail).

97. In addition to the usual emergency kit supplies (water, food, flashlight, batteries, medicine, etc.) the US Centers for Disease Control also suggests having these on hand for the zombie apocalypse and other disasters: matches, plastic sheeting, scissors, a wrench, pliers and – of course – the most versatile tool ever, duct tape.

98. Cures, quarantines or outposts of well-armed human survivors ... none of these would be enough to put a stop to the zombie apocalypse, conclude the Canadian researchers who published the study "When Zombies Attack! Mathematical Modelling of an Outbreak of Zombie Infection." Only a strategy called "impulsive eradication," where humans launch massive attacks, one after the other, could prevent the collapse of civilization, they say. That approach would allow people to destroy 25 percent of all zombies after two-and-a-half days, 50 percent after five days, 75 percent after seven-and-a-half days; and 100 percent after 10 days.

99. Since we're dealing with a horror-movie predator here, you should also follow the number-one survival rule from any film in that genre: don't split up from your group and go exploring on your own. Think about who's the first to go in any horror movie – it's always that guy or girl who says, "I'm going to go out to the garage/down to the basement/over to my neighbor's house for a minute. I'll be right back." Don't be that guy or girl.

100. More than anything else, though – at least if you're facing the regular, slow-moving zombies – it will pay to have done a lot of cardio workouts and be really fit when the zombie apocalypse arrives. As long as you can run faster than both the zombies and the rest of your friends, you'll be set.

BONUS CHAPTER: THE BEST WEBSITES ABOUT ZOMBIES

Centers for Disease Control and Prevention Zombie Novella (http://www.cdc.gov/phpr/zombies_novella.htm): This page provides links to downloadable and printable versions of "Preparedness 101: Zombie Pandemic," the CDC's fun graphic novel about a couple and their dog – Todd, Julie and Max – finding themselves in the middle of a zombie outbreak.

The Federal Vampire and Zombie Agency (http://fvza.org): Very tongue-in-cheek, this site features fictional tales and "histories" about zombie outbreaks, a virtual academy for self-defense against vampires and zombies, and various other odd links and resources.

The Guardian – Zombie Culture (http://www.theguardian.com/culture/zombies): A permanent feature of the British newspaper's website, this section provides regularly updated news about zombie culture: books, movies, TV shows and more.

Map of the Dead (http://www.mapofthedead.com/): This online guide lets you locate vital nearby resources in the event of a zombie apocalypse: campgrounds, doctor and dentist offices, gas stations, grocery stores, harbors, hardware stores, pharmacies and more. It also offers links and support for its companion iPhone survival game.

Plants vs. Zombies Wiki (http://plantsvszombies.wikia.com): A wiki encyclopedia about the video game Plants vs. Zombies, this site includes pictures and descriptions of every zombie in the game, from the relatively easy-to-kill regular day zombie to the tough and fearsome Giga-gargantuar zombie.

Reddit - Zombies (http://www.reddit.com/r/zombies): This subreddit's "raison de la mort" is to give zombie fans a place to share news, comments and questions about zombie books, games, gatherings, movies, music, speculative science and more.

Wikipedia (http://en.wikipedia.org/wiki/Zombie): As it is for almost any other topic, Wikipedia makes a good starting point for anyone interested in all things zombie. In addition to this general overview page about zombies, Wikipedia also features other pages with information on fictional zombies (as opposed to the other kind?), zombie films, zombie video games, "Night of the Living Dead," revenants, thanatology (the study of death) and Michael Jackon's classic "Thriller" video.

Zombie Neuroscience (http://cognitiveaxon.blogspot.com/search/label/zombies and http://blog.ketyov.com/2011/10/ zombie-brain.html): These two sites – The Cognitive Axon and Oscillatory Thoughts – are the blogging homes of, respectively, zombie-loving neuroscientist Tim Verstynen (assistant professor of psychology at Carnegie Mellon) and his fellow zombie-loving neuroscientist Bradley Voytek, assistant professor (as of early 2014) of computational cognitive science and neuroscience at the University of California-San Diego. While older material remains at his previous site, Verstynen now blogs at Psychology Today's White Matter Matters (http://www.psychologytoday.com/blog/white-matter-matters).

Zombie Research Society (http://www. zombieresearch.org): The (un)dead-serious Zombie Research Society was founded in 2007 by Matt Mogk, author of "Everything You Ever Wanted to Know About Zombies." Featuring news about zombie science, survival and culture, the ZRS advisory board includes "Night of the Living Dead" director George A. Romero, Harvard Medical School co-director of medical student education in psychiatry Steven Schlozman and neuroscientists/zombie fans Bradley Voytek and Timothy Verstynen.

Zombiepedia (http://zombie.wikia.com/wiki/Zombie_ Wiki): Zombiepedia describes itself as the only encyclopedia to "address the important subject of the undead, defense procedures during an outbreak, and scientific analysis of the zombie phenomenon." It has more than 700 pages covering categories from fan fiction and games to research and weapons.

Zombies on the Web (http://consc.net/zombies.html): Compiled by David Chalmers, professor of philosophy at Australian

National University and co-director of the Center for Mind, Brain and Consciousness at New York University, this site makes another good starting-off point for any zombie fan. Chalmers' amusing and eclectic content covers everything from the differences between Hollywood, Haitian and philosophical zombies; a comic strip with two dinosaurs discussing philosophy and zombies; and links to zombie movies, survival guides, trivia and voodoo terminology.

FOOTNOTES

1. Who First Thought of Zombies?

[i] Source: Zombiepedia, http://zombie.wikia.com/wiki/Zombies_in_folklore

[ii] Source: Man, Vol. 45, Mar - Apr 1945, Louis P. Mars, MD, "The Story of Zombi in Haiti," http://www.jstor.org/discover/10.2307/2792947?uid=3739600&uid=2&uid=4&uid=3739256&sid=21101563929691

2. Night of the Living Dead Animals

[iii] Source: Life's Little Mysteries, http://www.lifeslittlemysteries.com/2868-zombie-animals.html

[iv] Source: Miami Herald, http://www.miamiherald.com/2013/02/12/3230892/hacker-warns-of-zombies-on-2-mich.html

3. Rising from the Headlines

[v] Source: LiveScience, http://www.livescience.com/27287-zombie-apocalypse-world-war-ii.html

[vi] Source: Centers for Disease Control and Prevention, http://emergency.cdc.gov/preparedness/

[vii] Source: National Public Radio, http://www.npr.org/blogs/thetwo-way/2013/02/14/172019554/canada-to-zombies-drop-dead-eh

[viii] Source: The Providence Journal, http://news.providencejournal.com/breaking-news/2013/02/student-zombies-march-on-ri-department-of-education-in-protest.html

[ix] Source: The Guardian, http://www.guardian.co.uk/culture/zombies

[x] Source: Amazon, http://www.amazon.com/dp/1594743347

[xi] Source: Amazon, http://www.amazon.com/How-Make-Zombie-Science-

Reanimation/dp/1851689443/ref=sr_1_1?s=books&ie=UTF8&qid=13
74958772&sr=1-1

[xii] Source: Huffington Post, http://www.huffingtonpost.com/frank-swain/why-zombies-are-real_b_3461580.html

[xiii] Source: Death by Zombie!, http://deathbyzombie.com

[xiv] Source: New York Times, http://www.nytimes.com/2011/10/30/magazine/steve-jobs-vampire-bill-gates-zombie.html?pagewanted=2&_r=0

[xv] Source: Zombie Research Society, http://zombieresearchsociety.com/top-ten

[xvi] Source: Map of the Dead, http://www.mapofthedead.com

4. Zombie Tales

[xvii] Source: Palm Beach Post, http://www.palmbeachpost.com/news/travel/tne-things-i-learned-about-zombies-in-new-orleans/nYwY8/

[xviii] Source: Daily Sun: http://www.politicsweb.co.za/politicsweb/view/politicsweb/en/page71627?oid=393461&sn=Detail&pid=71616

[xix] Source: Living on Earth, http://loe.flyingsound.net/shows/shows.html?programID=08-P13-00052

[xx] Source: Yvette Brandy, http://ybrandyspeaks.com

[xxi] Source: *Wraiths, Revenants and Ritual in Medieval Culture*, Academia.edu, http://www.academia.edu/1515462/Wraiths_Revenants_and_Ritual_in_Medieval_Culture

[xxii] Source: *The Saga of Grettir the Strong*, http://www2.hn.psu.edu/faculty/jmanis/saga~gre/grettir.pdf

[xxiii] Source: Wikipedia, http://en.wikipedia.org/wiki/1935_Labor_Day_hurricane

[xxiv] Source: The Federal Vampire and Zombie Agency, http://www.fvza.org/topthree.html

[xxv] Source: Wikipedia, http://en.wikipedia.org/wiki/Clairvius_Narcisse

[xxvi] Source: Skeptoid, http://skeptoid.com/episodes/4262

[xxvii] JSTOR, "The Story of Zombi in Haiti," http://www.jstor.org/stable/2792947

5. The Science of Zombies

[xxviii] Source: Stanford University Center for the Explanation of Consciousness, http://csli-cec.stanford.edu/CECevents.html

[xxix] Source: PopSci, http://www.popsci.com/science/article/2013-02/fyi-would-zombies-be-conscious

[xxx] Source: University of Ottawa Press, http://www.presses.uottawa.ca/livre/braaaiiinnnsss

[xxxi] Source: London Science Museum, http://www.sciencemuseum.org.uk/about_us/press_and_media/press_releases/2013/01/zombielab.aspx

[xxxii] Source: https://share.sandia.gov/news/resources/news_releases/zombie-cells/

[xxxiii] Source: CNN, http://www.cnn.com/2012/07/11/health/uncanny-valley-robots/index.html

[xxxiv] Source: Wikipedia, http://en.wikipedia.org/wiki/Uncanny_valley

[xxxv] Source: Social Science Research Network, "Death and Taxes and Zombies," http://papers.ssrn.com/sol3/papers.cfm?abstract_id=2045255

[xxxvi] Source: "Rabid: A Cultural History of the World's Most Diabolical Virus," Powell's Books, http://www.powells.com/biblio/1-9780670023738-10

[xxxvii] Source: Wikipedia, http://en.wikipedia.org/wiki/Panspermia

[xxxviii] Source: Wired,

http://www.wired.com/wiredscience/2010/11/necropanspermia/

xxxix Source: Springer Link, http://link.springer.com/article/10.1007%2Fs11214-010-9671-x

6. Zombies at Play

xl Source: Plants vs. Zombies Wiki, http://plantsvszombies.wikia.com/wiki/Zombies

xli Source: Wikipedia, http://en.wikipedia.org/wiki/Thanatology

xlii Source: Wikipedia, http://en.wikipedia.org/wiki/Zombies_Ate_My_Neighbors

xliii Source: Telegraph, http://www.telegraph.co.uk/technology/video-games/Picture-galleries/8807859/The-20-Best-Zombie-Video-Games.html

xliv Source: Minecraft Wiki, http://www.minecraftwiki.net/wiki/Zombies

xlv Source: Wikipedia, http://en.wikipedia.org/wiki/Zombie_game

xlvi Source: About.com, http://classicgames.about.com/od/computergames/p/ZombieZombie.htm

xlvii Source: Zombies, Run! https://www.zombiesrungame.com/

xlviii Source: Wikipedia, http://en.wikipedia.org/wiki/Little_Red_Riding_Hood%27s_Zombie_BBQ

xlix Source: Telegraph, http://www.telegraph.co.uk/technology/video-games/Picture-galleries/8807859/The-20-Best-Zombie-Video-Games.html?image=19

7. Zombie Art

l Source: The Zombie Autopsies, http://thezombieautopsies.com/thebook

li Source: Amazon, http://www.amazon.com/Zombie-Haiku-Good-Poetry-Your-Brains/dp/1600610706/ref=pd_sim_b_4

[lii] Source: Wattpad, http://www.wattpad.com/story/2426517-the-happy-zombie-sunrise-home

[liii] Source: Telegraph, http://www.telegraph.co.uk/culture/books/booknews/9631421/Margaret-Atwood-QandA-the-zombie-apocalypse.html

[liv] Source: Figge Art Museum, http://thefigge.org/getdoc/a3e9812e-2b34-46c2-b4e8-34c1b038a2e1/B.aspx?page=4

[lv] Source: Archeology Magazine, http://archive.archaeology.org/online/interviews/zombies/

[lvi] Source: Fowler Museum at UCLA, http://www.fowler.ucla.edu/sites/default/files/curriculum/InExtremis_powerpoint_notes.pdf

[lvii] Source: Amazon, "Knit Your Own Zombie," http://www.amazon.com/Knit-Your-Own-Zombie-Combinations/dp/1440557160/ref=sr_1_1?s=books&ie=UTF8&qid=1375669929&sr=1-1

[lviii] Source: YouTube, https://www.youtube.com/watch?v=sOnqjkJTMaA

[lix] Source: Wikipedia, http://en.wikipedia.org/wiki/Michael_Jackson%27s_Thriller

[lx] Source: AMC TV, "The Walking Dead" makeup tips, http://www.amctv.com/shows/the-walking-dead/make-up-tips

[lxi] Source: Her Universe, http://www.heruniverse.com/brands/the-walking-dead.html

[lxii] Source: Villafane Studios, http://villafanestudios.com/

[lxiii] Source: The New York Botanical Garden, http://www.nybg.org/exhibitions/2012/halloween/index.php

8. Zombiewood

[lxiv] Source: Amazon, http://www.amazon.com/Rabid-Cultural-History-Worlds-Diabolical/dp/0670023736#reader_0670023736

lxv Source: Wikipedia, http://en.wikipedia.org/wiki/White_Zombie_%28film%29

lxvi Source: Wikipedia, http://en.wikipedia.org/wiki/Plan_9_from_Outer_Space

lxvii Source: Wikipedia, http://en.wikipedia.org/wiki/Zombie_%28fictional%29

lxviii Source: Wikipedia, http://en.wikipedia.org/wiki/Night_of_the_Living_Dead

lxix Source: Wikipedia: http://en.wikipedia.org/wiki/Living_Dead

lxx Source: BBC, http://www.bbc.co.uk/programmes/p00szzcm

lxxi Source, Greencine, http://www.greencine.com/static/primers/zombies1.jsp

lxxii Source: The Guardian, http://www.theguardian.com/commentisfree/2013/feb/08/warm-bodies-film-zombie-love-affair

lxxiii Source: Amazon, http://www.amazon.com/Attack-Vegan-Zombies-Christine-Egan/dp/B0038YX2DM

lxxiv Source: IMDB, http://www.imdb.com/title/tt2243469/?ref_=nv_sr_1

lxxv Source: IMDB, http://www.imdb.com/title/tt1623288/?ref_=nv_sr_1

lxxvi Source: BBC, http://www.bbc.co.uk/news/business-23931078

lxxvii Source: IMDB, http://www.imdb.com/title/tt2383382/

lxxviii Source: IMDB, http://www.imdb.com/title/tt2319871/

lxxix Source: The National Geographic Channel, http://channel.nationalgeographic.com/channel/episodes/the-truth-behind-zombies/

lxxx Source: Leeds Zombie Film Festival, http://leedszombiefilmfestival.com/

[lxxxi] Source: Zombie Feast Horror Film Festival, http://zombiefeast.ca/

[lxxxii] Source: Zompire, http://zompire.com/

[lxxxiii] Source: The Drunken Zombie Film Festival, http://drunkenzombiefilmfestival.com/

[lxxxiv] Source: Wikipedia, Zombie Walk, http://en.wikipedia.org/wiki/Zombie_walk

9. What Zombies can Teach Us

[lxxxv] Source: New Left Project, http://www.newleftproject.org/index.php/site/article_comments/what_zombie_films_can_teach_us_about_climate_change

[lxxxvi] Source: The Guardian, http://www.guardian.co.uk/commentisfree/2013/feb/11/americans-love-zombies-culture

[lxxxvii] Source: ABC News, http://www.abc2news.com/dpp/news/region/baltimore_county/facing-zombies-good-for-your-health

[lxxxviii] Source: STEM Behind Hollywood, a program created by Texas Instruments with the help of the Science & Entertainment Exchange at the National Academy of Sciences, http://education.ti.com/en/us/stem-hollywood/zombies

[lxxxix] Source: Harvard University, http://connects.catalyst.harvard.edu/Profiles/display/Person/3865

[xc] Source: Oscillatory Thoughts: The Zombie Brain, http://blog.ketyov.com/2011/10/zombie-brain.html

[xci] Source: The Cognitive Axon, http://cognitiveaxon.blogspot.com/search/label/zombies

[xcii] Source: The University of Buffalo, http://www.buffalo.edu/news/releases/2013/08/026.html

[xciii] Source: Amazon, http://www.amazon.com/John-Edgar-Browning/e/B002BOCCUO

[xciv] Source: The University of Essex, http://www.essex.ac.uk/news/event.aspx?e_id=5352

[xcv] Source: The University of Ottawa, http://mysite.science.uottawa.ca/rsmith43/Zombies.pdf

[xcvi] Source: Foreign Policy, http://www.foreignpolicy.com/articles/2013/07/15/history_of_the_world_part_z_zombies

[xcvii] Source: All Things Zombie, http://www.allthingszombie.com/mb/index.php?/topic/3146-how-can-zombies-possibly-rise-out-of-graves/

[xcviii] Source: Yahoo! Answers, http://answers.yahoo.com/question/index?qid=20110712012806AAdIKI5

10. Survival Tips for the Zombie Apocalypse

[xcix] Source: Quora, http://www.quora.com/Zombie-Apocalypse-Strategy/What-dont-people-do-in-zombie-apocalypse-movies-that-you-would-do

[c] Source: Quora, http://www.quora.com/Zombie-Apocalypse-Strategy/What-dont-people-do-in-zombie-apocalypse-movies-that-you-would-do

[ci] Source: The Weather Channel, http://www.weather.com/outlook/home-family/holidays/articles/zombie-apocalypse-weather_2011-10-11

[cii] Source: Map of the Dead, http://www.mapofthedead.com

Other freetothink book titles:

Prove It! Fact-Checking Secrets of a Fanatical Online Researcher (2014)

100 Ways to Make Money Online: A Guide to the 'Net's Top Freelance Marketplaces, Crowdsourcing Work Sites and Places to Sell Your Stuff (2012)

Rhythms of Shadow and Light in a Time of Divorce, Occupy and Climate Change (2012)

100 Cool Things About Bugs (2011)

For more information, visit freetothinkbooks.com

Copyright 2013, 2014 freetothinkbooks

freetothinkbooks.com

www.ingramcontent.com/pod-product-compliance
Lightning Source LLC
Chambersburg PA
CBHW061301040426
42444CB00010B/2455